for

David, Elliott and the Spirit that guides me

Rebecca

for

Gus, Ruth, Matthew and Cale

Mary

Sunny Spells, Scattered Showers

Rebecca Carroll and Mary Kennelly

Our sincere thanks go to:
Jo O'Donoghue – our editor, who didn't know what she was taking on but did it anyway
Valerie O'Sullivan – for her wonderful photographs
Bob Baker – for his invaluable advice in helping to select the paintings
Mary Cogan – for sifting through so many bad spellings
Rebecca's clients for surrendering up their paintings to be photographed
John Connolly, Gabriel Fitzmaurice, Mark Patrick Hederman and Kate O'Shea
for their time and kind words
Ann McAuliffe – for her tireless energy and support
Pierse and Fitzgibbon, solicitors, Listowel – for our very first cheque
Alison Healy and all at Tuatha Chiarrai – for making this project a whole lot easier
Our families and friends who put up with us along the way!
Without your help this book would have remained a dream.

Tuatha Chiarrai Teo  **National Rural Development Programme**

Project funded by the Irish government and part-financed by the European Union under the National Development Plan 2000–2006.

First edition
Published by Glenwood Books
2004
Glenwood Books, Glenwood Studio, Littor Strand, Asdee, Listowel, County Kerry, Ireland
email: glenwoodbooks@eircom.net

Artwork copyright © Rebecca Carroll and text copyright © Mary Kennelly
All rights reserved.
No part of this publication may be reproduced or transmitted in any form or by any means, electronic, mechanical, photocopy, recording or otherwise without prior permission of the copyright holders. Copyright protection will be strictly enforced by the publisher and the artists concerned.

ISBN 0–9546986–0–6

Designed by Rebecca Carroll
Cover Illustration *Soil Search* (2000) by Rebecca Carroll
Print origination by Carrigboy Typesetting Services, County Cork
Printed by GraphyCems, Villatuerta, Navarra, Spain.

Sunny Spells, Scattered Showers

Rebecca Carrolll and Mary Kennelly

Contents

Introduction	8
Foreword	9
Grace Descends – Rebecca's Prayer	10/11
Quiet Skeletons – Ogham	12/13
The Tree of Life – Scarred Oak	14/15
Orange Apple – Invitation to Dream	16/17
World-Mothering Air – Covenant	18/19
'I tell them there is no forgiveness and yet there is always forgiveness' – Scorched	20/21
Line Stone – Headstones	22/23
Mermaid's Purse – Mermaid	24/25
Cell – Miscarriage	26/27
Regatta 3 – Gale Force	28/29
Elliott's Effect – The Interview	30/31
Angel by My Side – Creation Story	32/33
Rebirth – Grace	34/35
Doorway 12, Elliott's – Elliott's Door	36/37
Nature's Dance – Afterglow	38/39
Saint Patrick's Purgatory – Last Things	40/41
Between Lands – Overseas	42/43
Nature's Cathedral – An Occasion of Sin	44/45
Irradiating – Love Story	46/47
Conquest – Conquest	48/49

Embryonic Atolls – Red Dreams	50/51
Tension 1&2 – The Hating	52/53
Love Me, Love Me Not – I Do Not Love You Any More	54/55
Transience – Orpheus and Eurydice	56/57
The Willow Weeps – Empire-Building	58/59
Whatever Was Turned Scarlet – Deconstruction	60/61
Trapped – Home in Time for Tea	62/63
Meeting Alan Erasmus – Lover's Hands	64/65
Bath in my Brain – Bath inside my Brain	66/67
Christmas Time – Ballylongford Via the North Pole	68/69
Garden of Eden – Eve	70/71
Doorway 1&2 – Encounter	72/73
Vortex of Fused Ideas – Seed Thrown into Thorn	74/75
Jacob's Ladder – Castle	76/77
Jinny Joes – Disappeared	78/79
Seer's Vision – The Seer	80/81
Rebecca's Daydream – Daydreams	82/83
Kissing the Dark – Maelstrom	84/85
Father's Journey – Liberation	86/87
Line, Light, Growth – Driving Blind	88/89
Forefather – Legacy	90/91
Soil Search – Soil Search	92/93
Biographies	94/95

Introduction

Every now and again, one opens a book that one will never forget – and this is one of them. It will appeal to women and men of all ages and any nationality as one reads between shape and line. Moreover, it is a book to be opened in a hayfield, park or beach, on a summer's day or over a fire in the depths of winter. Having spent most of my childhood in West Cork and Kerry, I recognise its 'mists' and nuances but also recognise that this book is unique in Irish feminist literature.

Conjured up between the leaves of these pages are the heart and soul of a modern Irishwoman, involved with family issues, yet fiercely independent in spirit and work. Springing out of Kerry, Mary Kennelly's poetry – imbued with simplicity, yet straight to the point – combined with the unique textured and spatial vision of Rebecca Carroll's colourful and extraordinary painting, is a sensual feast to be approached and savoured.

For artists living and breathing in a similar environment and culture, linking painting and poetry in this way is akin to putting body and soul together. Is it only women who are rooted in emotions? A human condition survives anywhere, it would seem. Such culture can combine naturalism and symbolism and for the art historian and literary critic theoretical debates ensue constantly as to the merits or drawbacks of any kind of categorisation. Nonetheless, in this instance, compare the simple lines of Kennelly's 'Invitation to Dream' with those of Carroll's 'Orange Apple'. Both are rooted in a form of naturalism. Again, extend this contrast to the rhythms of 'Maelstrom' in unison with an exploration of oil on the canvas of 'Kissing the Dark' – all the while fathoming emotions and psychology rooted in symbolism.

Then turn back to focus on the works of poets such as Eavan Boland, Medbh McGuckian, Moyra Donaldson and on visual artists such as Camille Souter, Carol Graham and Rita Duffy, working in similar and alternate veins of womanhood and one begins to see a landscape which Mary Kennelly and Rebecca Carroll share with these Irishwomen.

Enjoy this book because it talks about the present. All true art lives there and others consign history to it. 'A new world calls for a new man', Yves Klein, the French visual artist, said in the 1950s. I would be inclined to say 'New worlds call for new women' – and Kennelly and Carroll are already there.

    Dr. Kate O'Shea
    Art historian and critic
    Belfast, 2004

FOREWORD

While at an exhibition of Rebecca's paintings during 2002, I spotted a small dark painting with one illuminating source of light. There was something about the painting, entitled *Grace Descends*, which drew me in and captivated me; I was genuinely disappointed to find that the painting was not for sale. Later on that evening, while in Rebecca's company, I mentioned the painting to her; she explained that for her it represented the spirituality of creativity. In a gesture typical of her she decided that if the painting meant so much to me I was meant to have it and she gave it to me as a gift! A few weeks later, while working on something else, the poem 'Rebecca's Prayer' found its way on to the page. I gave the poem to Rebecca and in that simple exchange of gifts lay the genesis of this book.

I first met Rebecca while working on the committee of the Brendan Kennelly Summer Festival and as our relationship developed into friendship, I found her to be startlingly honest, artistically generous and confidently optimistic. Frequently we spoke about our work and shared ideas and this led, at times, to an influence on each other's work. Eventually we took the decision to take our work together a stage further.

The process of working so closely with another person was challenging and at times difficult. There were occasions when I began to wonder if I would ever have another independent thought that was not in someway influenced or scrutinised by Rebecca and I know she felt the same way. But the work was also immensely satisfying and exciting as we explored themes such as nature, spirituality, love, family, loss, sex, death and our sense of place. We worked by sharing ideas and obsessions; sometimes the painting came first, sometimes the poem, sometimes they were born simultaneously and sometimes one or other of us could not follow where the other had led.

Through our collaboration together, Rebecca and I have grown and we will carry the results of that growth with us in all our future work. This book details that collaboration – we hope you enjoy it!

Mary Kennelly

REBECCA'S PRAYER

Blank canvas forcing new beginnings,
Emptiness demanding, challenging courage
And God given gifts.

The artist's steely eye
Tempered by sympathetic ear,
Colours surging beyond vision into soul.

Soul scraped painfully inch by inch,
Exposed now for all the world to see.
A perfect painting? Her perfect prayer.

GRACE DESCENDS
Oil on board, *26 x 34cm, 2002*

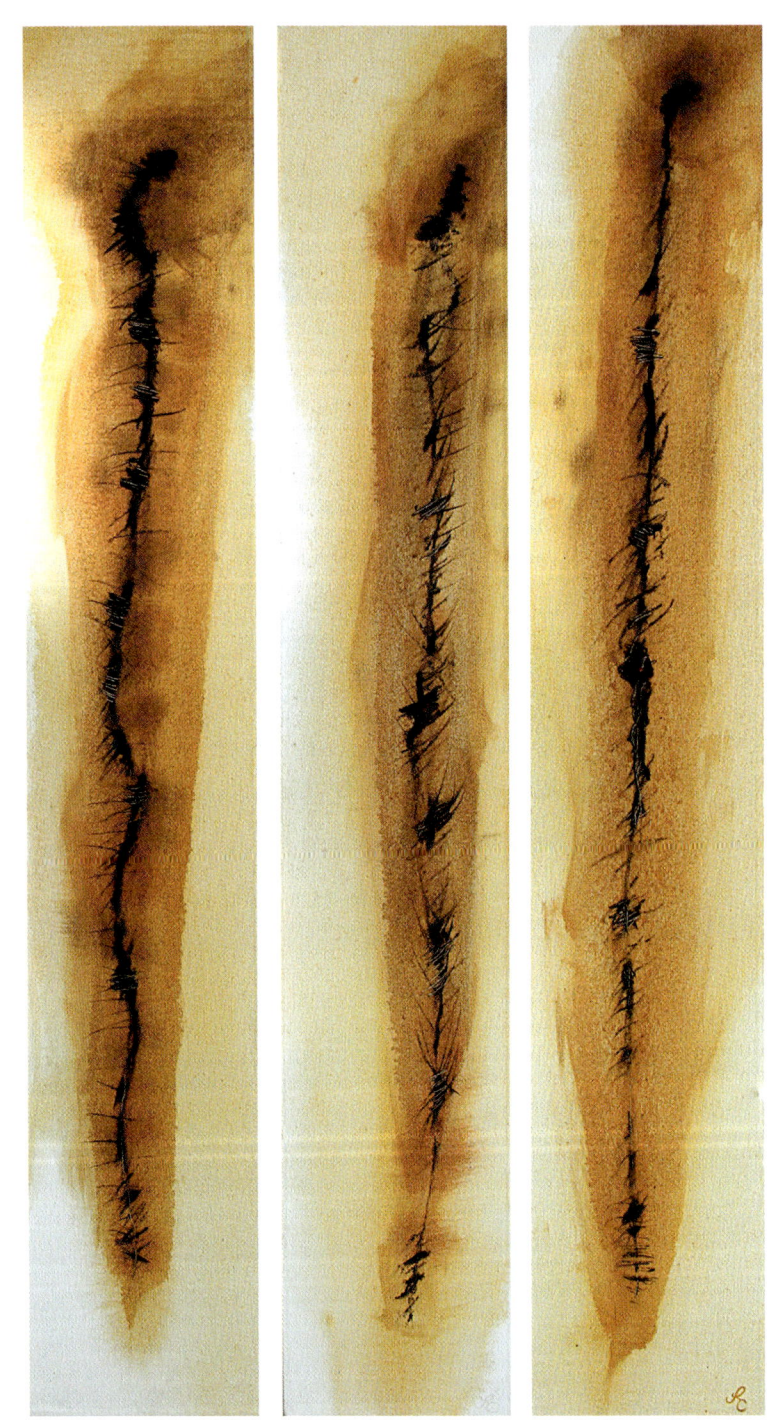

Ogham

His people lived in story.

His story is sacrificed to stone.

I do not know his hair or eyes,

How he laughed, if he danced

Or carried music in his voice.

The stones will tell me only that

His father-king has grieved for him.

However long I stand and stare

The lines are quiet skeletons.

Nothing else remains.

Once he lived and he was loved.

Quiet Skeletons
Oil on canvas, *60 x 122cm, triptych, 2003*

Scarred Oak

The druids understood the magic of my kind.

What would they have made of me

Fed on rock and salt water –

A small, twisted, wreckage of a tree?

I do not know when wanting changed to needing

And needing then began to gnarl my bark and branch.

I have seen a century of storm and death

And widows' tears enough to swell the sea.

Lovers' lies whispered softly as a kiss,

Seasons, sunshine, showers.

I know nothing but wood and sky and sea.

I know everything that can be known to me.

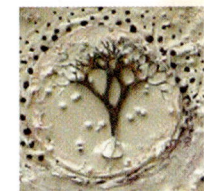

The Tree of Life
Mixed media on panel, *64 x 64cm, 2000*

INVITATION TO DREAM

She brought the invitation home

And for one never-ending week

She had to wait . . .

Who knew what strange delights

Might be on show at Claudia's

All-girl, dress-up, birthday party?

Orange apples, pink bananas,

Chocolate chairs and magic drinking cups,

A living breathing birthday cake?

Wonderland for all five-year-olds,

If Friday would just come!

ORANGE APPLE
Pastels, mixed media on panel, *56 x 57cm, 1998*

Covenant

I feel you move and of its own accord
My hand flies down to cradle you.
Idle thoughts drift to what the future holds
For me and you – a child I love as no one else,
Whose face as yet I do not know.
I move spellbound through my hopes for us,
Dreading the tears that loving you might bring,
Fearful too of somehow failing you.
But in the end, my unborn child,
All that I have been and done before,
My life itself, a training ground for this –
My greatest triumph, my saving grace,
Is loving and being loved by you.

WORLD-MOTHERING AIR
Oil on board, *92 x 66cm, 2002*

"I tell them there is no forgiveness, and yet there is always forgiveness"
Oil on canvas, *70 x 330cm, triptych, 2003*

SCORCHED

I am with him in everything he does
And yet he is ashamed of me,
The mention of my name out loud
Is enough to make him tremble.
He hides me deeply as he can,
As if I were a creature of the light.
He vows that he will master me.
He pretends he does not know
That I am safest in the dark.
It's there I grow and gain in strength
And there I lie in wait for him,
Then in his quiet times
I struggle and break free.
When I am out he tastes me,
Hates himself but loves me.
I stretch myself across his skin,
I scorch his every nerve
Until he lies,
Seduced, spent, shivering.

HEADSTONES

Silently, the woman walked the shoreline.

No sound, save the Atlantic's

Whispered kiss upon the rocks,

To distract her from her task.

She must find the perfect stone.

Some she raised and stroked

But at length they were discarded,

Until at last she found the one

To be the headstone for her child

– The baby lost too soon to have a grave.

The stone would rest securely in her bedroom,

To be the focus of her tears.

And every night she'd softly lay her touch

On her three children sleeping in their beds

And five headstones on a graveyard windowsill.

LINE STONE
Oil, mixed media on panel, *64 x 64cm, 2000*

MERMAID

She wants to be a teacher
And a mummy just like me.
But she will be a mermaid too
And spend her time at sea.
And every day, she promises,
She'll pop up and have a chat,
To let me know about the kids
And work and things like that.
And however wide the ocean,
She'll gently swim across.
I can even come to tea one day,
If I'm feeling at a loss.
"But you said that you would be a vet
And work at Dublin zoo."
She sighs and throws her eyes to God:
"Oh Mummy, I can do that too!"

MERMAID'S PURSE
Mixed media on panel, *42 x 82cm, 2001*

Cell

Oil, wax on panel, *31 x 38 cm, 2002*

MISCARRIAGE

What does it matter
What you say,
What I say,
What I want,
What he wants,
What the doctors do?
Tests, scans, injections,
I.V.I., I.V.F.
In the end it comes to this –
I have flushed four pregnancies
Down the toilet,
In the building where I work.

detail

REGATTA 3
Oil on canvas, *53.5 x 305cm, 2001*

GALE FORCE

The boy wears his father's face,
With nothing more of mine
Than the colour of his eyes.
Still, when the fearsome gales blew in,
Murdering Indian summer,
Spitting winter chill at us,
He came with me.
In coats that almost kept us warm
We sat and watched, with our same eyes,
The grey Atlantic bare white teeth
And rage against the whipping wind.
His small hand wrapped tight in mine,
Sharing – who can say?
Perhaps, in the end, no more than
The simple joy of watching nature's canvas
And being some small part of it.

Elliott's Effect
Mixed media on panel, *37 x 119cm, 2001*

THE INTERVIEW
(Cale at three weeks)

His misery is given full expression,

He roars out his displeasure,

Skin once alabaster turns mottled red.

Apologetically I rush to pick him up,

My touch enough for ceasefire.

His eyes now seeking mine

— Interrogation time.

Then, deciding I will do,

He turns and drinks his fill.

CREATION STORY
(*For Ruth*)

Until I held you I was many things –
Daughter, sister, lover.
When I looked on you, a thing apart,
You turned me into mother.

Your newborn, ancient, piercing eyes
Searched through mine, into soul.
You gathered all that I had been
And somehow made me whole.

My desperate need to keep you safe
Led to fear without cessation.
But in you I touched the face of God
– My daughter, My creation.

ANGEL BY MY SIDE
Acrylics, mixed media on panel, *81 x 81cm, 1999*

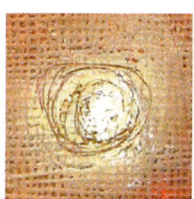

GRACE

Since yesterday the sound of quiet weeping.
She packs her bag for Holles Street.
At thirty-three he goes to buy a grave.
Now the silence marks them out.
No laughing questions on her future,
No promised happy ending to seven months of plans.
Instead, the midwives offer gentle consolation.

Then the moment of her birth,
A split-second greeting and goodbye.
But time stands still in deference to her.
She fills the room with overwhelming peace.
Then tenderly, before they bring her home,
They name their daughter
For her most precious gift to them.

REBIRTH
Oil on board, *23 x 30cm, 2002*

ELLIOTT'S DOOR

The door called to him, promising adventure

In the forbidden room beyond.

The tantalising smells of turpentine,

Linseed oil and paint,

Begging him to make his mark,

On the floor, the walls, his mother's work.

So he went through and found

A door beyond the door,

Emerging out of dreamy blue.

Unable to resist its call,

He reached out, touched it,

And fell into dreams.

DOORWAY 12 – ELLIOTT'S
Oil and pigment on canvas, *40 x 56cm, 2003*

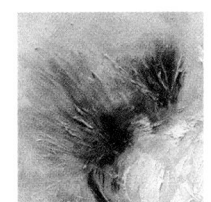

AFTERGLOW

Spent from nature's oldest dance, we lie,
Bones not yet returned to solid form,
Utterly familiar and content,
Alive but insulated from our daily cares,
And shortly dreams will come in sleep.

NATURE'S DANCE
Oil on canvas, *59 x 59cm, 2001*

Saint Patrick's Purgatory
Oil on canvas, *84 x 178cm, 2003*

LAST THINGS

In one devastating flash of blue-white heat
You travelled to that place
Where death and life make love.
And we held fast, despite our fears,
To a tiny desperate hope,
While you faced bravely
The four last things –
Death, Judgement, Heaven, Hell.
Then in the end,
Our cries drowned out by angel song,
You left.
And we, the ones you left behind,
With flowers, weeping, prayer and earth,
Began the purgatory of letting go.

Between Lands
Oil on board, *triptych, 38 x 62cm, 2002*

OVERSEAS

Tonight he is away from me

And from the life we share,

From tragic tales of schoolyard woes

And dinnertime's shared laughter,

From bedtime stories, one last drinks

And precious slurpy kisses.

Tonight I lie alone in bed – our bed,

Pleasure palace, tempest, theatre of dreams.

I know the world may never number us

Among its greatest lovers,

But tonight he is away from me

And I miss him, somewhere,

Deep within my bones.

An Occasion of Sin

It's beyond all understanding,
If He did not wish our sin,
That God should put upon this earth,
Perfection such as him,
To ignite the schoolgirl hormones
That we had thought long dead,
Putting images of taste and touch
And tempest in our heads.
While our poor foolish husbands
Ran up and down some more,
Delighted that we'd come to watch
And cheer their latest score,
We entertained ourselves throughout
Dreaming games played in his bed.
Respectability be dammed,
We were married but not dead.
And perhaps our sin was really prayer
And our illicit thrill
Was nothing more when seen close up
Than admiration of God's skill.

Nature's Cathedral
Graphite on paper, *62 x 93cm, 1999*

IRRADIATING
Oil and wax on canvas, *38 x 66cm, 2003*

LOVE STORY

This is not the kind of love
I dreamed of as a girl,
This ordinary, everyday,
Constant sort of love.
There are no daily diamonds or champagne,
No twenty-four red rose bouquets.
This love runs through little seams,
Folding clothes and sweeping floors.
Passion in a thousand tender acts.

Conquest
Oil on canvas, *61 x 183cm, triptych, 2003*

CONQUEST

He takes what he wants,
He rises, proud, majestic, dominant.

She lies beneath,
Acquiescent silk swallows steel.

He sets the pace,
Pummelling, punishing, pleasuring?

She bends to his will,
Her body driven on by his.

Rhythm grows past his control,
Ensnared, he can't turn back.

Her body hums its magic
She allows its warmth to spread.

A universe explodes from him,
He lies emptied and shivering.

Filled, she comes to life,
With all that she has taken from him.

Embryonic Atolls
Mixed media on panel, *54 x 70cm, 1999*

RED DREAMS

Not caring how she came to be
Among these people, in this place,
She felt the drumbeat and firelight dancing
Infuse the tent, the earth, the air with life.
Unbidden, her feet began to move,
Hips answering a pulse as old as time itself.
Then he was there – black hair, black eyes, red skin.
She took his hand and youth returned in dance,
Loving through eyes and hips and hands.
Living beauty – until the anaesthetic waned,
Forcing cold reality, leaving her bereft.
No tent, no brave, no youth, no womb.

Tension 1 & 2
Oil, mixed media on two panels, *17 x 44cm, 2001*

THE HATING

Slowly it began, at first with words
Like family and bleeding and infertility.
Then I let it flow to fools who asked
When we would fill our empty rooms
With children of our own.
And finally it came to rest on her,
My one-time dearest friend,
When her youngest child was born.

I fed it when she came to call,
Lamenting lost nights' sleep
But it grew fiercely of its own
When she laughed her joy in him.
Her breastfeeding became to me
A vulgar victory dance.
Then tenderly I began to nurture it,
As any mother would her child.

Steadily, steadily, it grew,
Until I could not stand to breathe the air
If she walked into the room.
I cut her roughly from my life,
I saw her baffled tears,
And I could not help rejoicing
That I had given birth, at last,
To such a powerful thing.

I Do Not Love You Any More

I do not love you any more; in fact I am no longer sure

If that young excited buzz I felt, for a little while

So long ago, was ever love at all.

But if it was – it is no more.

You did not beat me or drink too much,

You never were unfaithful or knowingly unkind,

And you will not understand why, after all this time,

I leave because I cannot bear to stay.

Let's just say, my love was massacred by little things

Like your politics, the clothes you wear,

And that sound you make when drinking tea.

LOVE ME, LOVE ME NOT
Mixed media on panel, *63 x 63cm, 1999*

TRANSIENCE
Oil and pigment on panels, *triptych, 23 x 90cm, 2001*

ORPHEUS AND EURYDICE

Though church bells' rhythm still rang in his ears,
Perhaps it was not simply passion's heat
That spurred him on to face
The terrors of the underworld alone.
No, surely it was something more –
A thing so seeming colourless,
Next to passion's great displays,
A deeper, quieter, stronger love,
That on her leaving
Stripped all joyous notes from him,
Leaving piteous sounds to tear
Compassion from dreaded Hades
And his pomegranate-poisoned Persephone.
A wound to move the underworld itself.
Such great love, almost to win the day,
Betrayed only by passion's insecurity.

EMPIRE-BUILDING

I could not stand their suffering to go unknown
And so I watched as Al Jezzera
Ran pictures of a tiny headless corpse,
A grotesque parody of the Allies'
Promised decapitation strike.
There were pictures too of frightened
Boys and a girl – nineteen-year-old cannon fodder,
Prisoners of war and fate.
Do politicians' children fight in wars?
Do politicians?

In the morning, punch-drunk and tarnished
By the horror in my sitting room,
I sank my hands into honest dirt.
I needed to forget their powerlessness and mine,
So I did the only thing I could – I prayed,
And planted spring cabbage and sweet peas
To remind me of the people of Mesopotamia.

THE WILLOW WEEPS
Oil on canvas, *30 x 30cm, 2003*

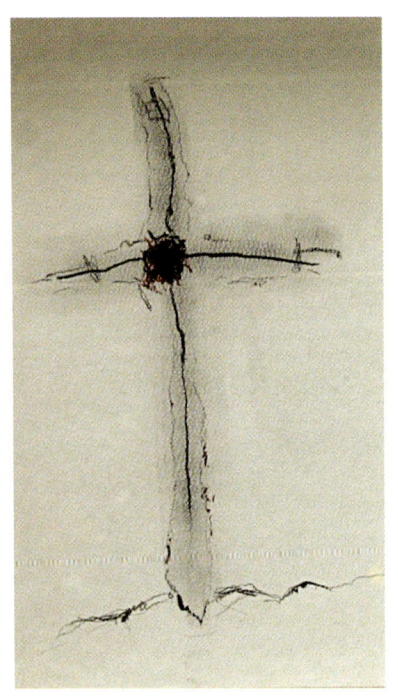  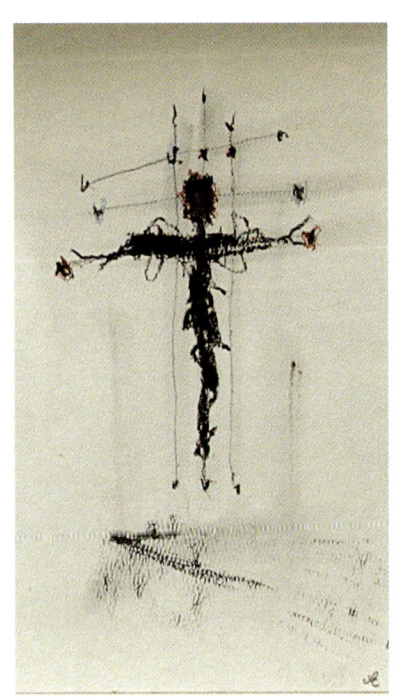

WHATEVER WAS TURNED SCARLET
Oil and graphite on paper, *39 x 70cm, 2003*

DECONSTRUCTION

Everything that once blazed scarlet

Is now the grey abyss

Of a body in irreversible decay.

Terror grows behind his eyes,

Desperation is his final hurt,

Making every day a crucifixion.

His faith is hardest tested in the space

Where trust and fear wage war,

And he is left with only this:

Perhaps You do exist,

Perhaps he will find rest.

Suffer little children to come unto You?

TRAPPED
Oil on canvas, *28 x 48cm, 2000*

HOME IN TIME FOR TEA

Even as a child I sometimes
Yearned to be alone.
I ran away from home with all the
Drama such events require,
Disgusted at my mother's ringing taunt,
"You'll be home in time for tea".
Today I ran away from home again,
No children dressed, no shopping done,
My mobile phone switched off,
Destination – me!
And now I wonder if you're wondering
If I've run away for good –
Seduced, perhaps, by irresponsibility.
Well, not to worry, love,
Six hours of total silence does the trick
And it seems that I remain the same,
 I'll still be home in time for tea.

LOVER'S HANDS

She is ashamed of them –
Big, rough-skinned and broken-nailed.
She wears gloves to cover them
Whenever she goes out,
Unaware how simply they speak
Words that I have never heard her say.
Every single callous earned from
Lifting, dressing, washing and the like,
A silent testament of her love for him.

MEETING ALAN ERASMUS
Mixed media on panel, *82 x 82cm, 1999*

BATH INSIDE MY BRAIN

I'd like to take a bath

Inside my brain,

To splash around and spill out

All the sludgy browns

Of living day to day,

And then the black

Of countless cruelties,

Meant and unintentional.

I'd sail through

Passion's blinding reds,

To brighter shores

And gentler hues.

I'd indulge a light flirtation

With the creature that is me,

And I'd learn to dance

A joyous dance

With unfettered creativity.

BATH IN MY BRAIN
Oil on canvas, *30 x 30cm, 2003*

CHRISTMAS TIME
Oil on board, *19 x 19cm, 2002*

BALLYLONGFORD VIA THE NORTH POLE

On Christmas Eve we go
To Nana Bally's house,
Stopping here and there to gaze
At winter wonderlands of lights,
Santas, snowmen, reindeer sleighs.
We come to share a parent's joy
In children's Christmas rapture,
When that first distant bell is heard.
For with that simple tinkling sound
All urbane pretence is stripped away,
Mums and dads – now children too.
Hearts swell because he's here.

The door opens to his knock.
He comes bringing little gifts,
Instructions to go straight to bed,
And magic to our world.
Our children wide-eyed and entranced
By one extraordinary neighbour's
Christmas pilgrimage of joy.
Before he turns to go,
This year, as every year,
I am five years old again
Dancing rings of bliss because
Tonight, at last, he comes!
And it no longer matters
If the stuffing is not made,
Or the house is not quite straight.
– Christmas has begun.

GARDEN OF EDEN
Oil on canvas, *triptych, 23 x 69cm, 2003*

EVE

Only the castle stones understand how

For the love of his eyes, his voice, his hands,

I lit my small light and let in the dark

To hang every last soul; not just the men,

But those bowed by age

And those still innocent in youth,

And women, silently weeping – all died for my need.

One spat in my face and cried 'Magdalene!'

Strange, is it not, to name me for she who

Did not run away but stayed to the end,

Who washed His feet with her tears?

They had better to name me for Eve

Who betrayed paradise, gave birth

To men's death and was lured into hell.

DOORWAY *1 & 2*
Oil, graphite and wax on two panels, *40 x 100cm, 2001*

ENCOUNTER

So do you write yourself?

What is it that you write?

I don't like all these new poems.

They don't rhyme any more.

I wrote a poem once,

I entered it in a competition,

It didn't do any good,

It rhymed,

And I didn't take a course.

I'm taking a great course now –

Creative writing,

Advanced.

It's better than poetry anyhow.

VORTEX OF FUSED IDEAS
Oil, graphite and wax on three panels, *triptych*, 16.5 x 49.5cm, 2001

SEED THROWN INTO THORN

It was my favourite, so at the beginning
Of each year I read it out for them,
The sower and the seed.
And I believed your seed had found a rich black earth in me.
No war or death or cruelty could overwhelm
The gift of faith you'd sown.
Oh Qoheleth, you do well to laugh at me!

Even what they did to the children,
Could not keep me from your house.
But did you see your chosen ones,
Lie and cheat, declare false bankruptcy,
To protect Holy Mother Church's things?
Cephas betrayed for greed beyond Judas.
And Christ, where were you in all of this?

Enraged, I closed my heart and banished you.
Now like Eve, the first separated,
Naked, terrified, alone, an infinitely lesser
Being for the loss of you, I cry,
A voice in the wilderness, seeking
Not understanding but faith.

Castle

I know what draws you here to me

And why you lift your face

To greet the gentle mist as friend.

You understand that dreams flow up and down

On the tide that soaks my stone.

A thousand times a thousand dreams now share this rock

With the ghosts of those who were betrayed.

This is why you slowly climb

My hundred twisting steps

And struggle, out of breath, until

You break into the light.

I am more to you than

Stone and stairs and sea,

For this is where you come,

To hear your darkest dreams –

Pleading to be let fly

Or else to be set free.

JACOB'S LADDER
Oil on canvas, *55 x 82cm, 2002*

JINNY JOES
Oil on board, *19 x 27cm, 2000*

Disappeared
(*For JoJo*)

The painting made me think of you.

Bog's bleakness defeated by wild flowers.

I think of your struggle to get safe home,

A shy smile at one you thought might rescue you.

You stepped innocently into nothingness,

A black hole of silence left behind

To torture those who found their joy in you.

It sends them out to search in every stranger's

Face they see for an answer – or a reason,

Dark dreams wound with images of all that might have passed.

I had forgotten them, and you, until

The picture bade me spare the time to weave a prayer,

That in whatever bleak and barren spot you rest,

Wild flowers bloom and whisper tenderness to you.

Seer's Vision
Oil on canvas, *26 x 143cm, 2002*

The Seer

Unbidden, sometimes unwelcome,
The mists would part and clear
As she was given sight denied to most,
A hand of light that reached for her
And claimed her for God's own.
Or the grey forgotten ones
That came one night,
Bringing dread deep in her bones,
The touch of angel's breath on skin,
Visions of the world from outside in.

DAYDREAMS

He stopped to admire my work,

Or so he said,

And, if I did not mind,

To offer – just a little – criticism.

My mouth stayed shut,

My brain took off,

I enjoyed my first garrotting.

REBECCA'S DAYDREAM
Oil on board, *26 x 34cm, 2002*

MAELSTROM

It rises, driven from the deep
By the thousand constant noises
That will not let it sleep.
Awoken, tracking every moving thing
And fierce enough to eat its young,
What is left for it to do but run
– Beyond the sounds of man –
To where, at length, the sea sings
Peace into its restless dark?
Then – slowly creeping in with quiet – old sounds
And half-forgotten songs return,
Soft as any lover's touch,
For out of silence, story is reborn.

KISSING THE DARK
Oil on canvas, *23 x 23cm*, *2001*

LIBERATION

God's graces are most strangely given,

Beyond our skills to reason.

Though body failed him day by day,

Still spirit soared in flight.

"Last night," he said, "I dreamt I walked,

'Till morning brought home truth,

But enough of that –

Today was good,

I'm glad I lived to see it."

FATHER'S JOURNEY
Oil, mixed media on panel, *64 x 64cm, 2001*

LINE, LIGHT, GROWTH
Oil, wax on panel, *30 x 38cm, 2002*

DRIVING BLIND

We woke from restless sleep to answer
The call we had been waiting for,
The call our hearts could not accept must come.
Fumbling to gather up our clothes and wits,
We left my mother to guard our children,
Sleeping undisturbed in bed.

We drove almost blind through greedy fog,
Opening resentfully in front of us,
Swallowing whole all that we had left behind.
We didn't talk; we didn't even want to think,
Needing to pretend that all was well,
Despite the way our blood refused to warm.

He accepted, as we could not,
That we were there to say goodbye,
His faith ensuring fear was ours alone;
He was simply travelling on.

Later, when our world had changed,
We drove home, unsure, through fog.
Too tired to dwell on tomorrow's intricate details,
The past unravelling behind us, now that
The clay from where his clay was drawn had gone,
Clutching, white-knuckled, to each other and today.

Forefather
Oil on canvas, *triptych, 46 x 138cm, 2003*

LEGACY

In time, you'll come to see
Your mother's eyes in your shaving mirror
And you'll hear your father's laughter
Echoed in your own.
Talk of how your uncle played that game before
Will make you grit your teeth to know
That you were not the first.
But will you ever spare a thought
For those in county Clare
Whose tongues once loved the tune you sing?
Or ever come to realise
That when you speak those words,
To draw my smile,
Mary-Ellen Finucane
And Ned FitzMaurice
Once used that turn of phrase?
Will you have to journey out
To other shores before you understand,
How those who picked
Periwinkles and sea grass
To quiet a savage hunger
Are why your heart is never easy
Unless it hears the sea?
And why grey stone washed
By water always seems to
Whisper 'Welcome home!'

SOIL SEARCH

Stretching deep into you,
Sucking everything I need
To blossom and amaze,
I stand and am admired.
To you alone I show the me
I hide from everybody else –
My darker, wilder, pagan parts.
And constant in those depths,
Where we are almost one,
Is your black earth,
A hidden source that births
The gentler things in me.

SOIL SEARCH
Oil, mixed media on panel, *45 x 45cm, 2000*

Rebecca Carroll

Born on 13 May 1964 in County Kerry, Rebecca spent her childhood between her home town of Listowel and the shores of the Shannon estuary – a coastal area known as Littor Strand. It was here, surrounded by woodland and the sounds of the sea, that she felt most at ease. Painting and photographing these surrounds were a happy part of her childhood. The spiritual and natural essence of this area was to play an important role in her future.

Rebecca studied visual communications in her foundation year at the Limerick College of Art and Design, followed by two years of photography at Kevin Street College of Technology, Dublin. After some time travelling, she returned to Limerick to complete her National Diploma in Design.

Following eight years as a graphic designer with RTE television in Dublin, she returned home to north Kerry in 1998. She has set up a home, studio and gallery beside her beloved Littor Strand. Rebecca lives with her husband David and son Elliott.

Rebecca has been painting prolifically since 1999, creating to date over 300 paintings shown within nine solo shows and sixteen group exhibitions in Ireland and the UK. Her work is predominantely held in private collections in Ireland; more recently her work is being purchased by American and UK clients.

She has been the visual arts coordinator for the Brendan Kennelly Summer Festival since the festival began in 2000, and through this work she formed a friendship with Mary Kennelly. 'When I first met Mary I was taken by her use of vocabulary. I saw her articulation as a gift. I find the conversations between us rewarding, amusing and at times wise. There is something in the give and take of these conversations that just plain gives. I am happy to have journeyed with Mary on this project for the past year.'

Rebecca says 'The essence of my work depicts nature and spirituality. The works are created spontaneously from the subconscious. It is as if someone is guiding me and at times I know this presence to be the Holy Spirit. I believe that my work has a healing effect not only for myself but also for the viewer. I paint for myself and for the messages that people receive from my work. Some people feel a sense of peace when they stay with a painting for just that moment longer.

Everyone is individual and if a painting appeals to someone, I believe, it is because there is a quality in that painting which is a reflection of the viewer themselves.

I feel privileged to be an artist and consider it a noble ministry.'

Mary Kennelly

Born in County Kerry in 1970, she was raised in the village of Ballylongford: 'The Kerry of my childhood was a place filled with unique characters, colourful stories and a landscape firmly imprinted with the ghosts of the past.' From an early age she has had a great love of history and mythology nurtured, in no small part, by the castles, churches and great houses that are scattered throughout the north Kerry landscape. 'Carrigafoyle Castle and Lislaughtin Abbey were the physical manifestations of enthralling stories, stories of heroes and heroines, of power and betrayal, of courage and loss.'

Mary studied Theology and History at St. Patrick's College, Maynooth, and later took a Higher Diploma in Education at University College, Galway. In 1993 she returned to Kerry to take up a teaching position in the Presentation Secondary School, Listowel. Since then she has been involved in many areas of the arts. She served as chairperson of Listowel Writer's Week from 1996 to 1999. She was a founder member of the Brendan Kennelly Summer Festival and has worked as Arts Director to the festival since its inception in 1999. She has written features for a number of publications including the *Kerryman*, the *Sunday Independent* and the *Sunday Tribune*. She has also edited a number of publications. She now lives on the north Kerry–west Limerick border with her husband Gus and her children Ruth, Matthew and Cale.

She has written since childhood but struggled for many years with a strong reluctance to write poetry. 'Following in the footsteps of one family member can seem daunting and the notion of writing poetry when both my father and my uncle are published writers has always seemed vaguely insane, but there is something involuntary about writing – like the persistent knocking on a door which, when finally opened, reveals a welcome friend.'

She has found working with Rebecca Carroll a challenging but immensely rewarding experience. *Sunny Spells, Scattered Showers* is Mary's first book.